foundations
SMALL GROUP STUDY

taught by tom Holladay and kay warren

SALVATION

 ZONDERVAN®

SADDLEBACK CHURCH

ZONDERVAN.com/
AUTHORTRACKER
follow your favorite authors

Foundations: *Salvation Study Guide*
Copyright © 2003, 2004, 2008 by Tom Holladay and Kay Warren

Requests for information should be addressed to:
Zondervan, *Grand Rapids, Michigan* 49530

ISBN 978-0-310-27682-1

08 09 10 11 12 13 14 15 16 17 18 • 23 22 21 20 19 18 17 16 15 14 13 12 11 10 9 8 7 6 5 4 3 2 1

foundations TABLE OF CONTENTS

FOREWORD

What *Foundations* Will Do for You

I once built a log cabin in the Sierra mountains of northern California. After ten backbreaking weeks of clearing forest land, all I had to show for my effort was a leveled and squared concrete foundation. I was discouraged, but my father, who built over a hundred church buildings in his lifetime, said, "Cheer up, son! Once you've laid the foundation, the most important work is behind you." I've since learned that this is a principle for all of life: you can never build *anything* larger than the foundation can handle.

The foundation of any building determines both its size and strength, and the same is true of our lives. A life built on a false or faulty foundation will never reach the height that God intends for it to reach. If you skimp on your foundation, you limit your life.

That's why this material is so vitally important. *Foundations* is the biblical basis of a purpose-driven life. You must understand these life-changing truths to enjoy God's purposes for you. This curriculum has been taught, tested, and refined over ten years with thousands of people at Saddleback Church. I've often said that *Foundations* is the most important class in our church.

Why You Need a Biblical Foundation for Life

- *It's the source of personal growth and stability.* So many of the problems in our lives are caused by faulty thinking. That's why Jesus said the truth will set us free and why Colossians 2:7a (CEV) says, *"Plant your roots in Christ and let him be the foundation for your life."*

- *It's the underpinning of a healthy family.* Proverbs 24:3 (TEV) says, *"Homes are built on the foundation of wisdom and understanding."* In a world that is constantly changing, strong families are based on God's unchanging truth.

- *It's the starting point of leadership.* You can never lead people farther than you've gone yourself. Proverbs 16:12b (MSG) says, *"Sound leadership has a moral foundation."*

- *It's the basis for your eternal reward in heaven.* Paul said, *"Whatever we build on that foundation will be tested by fire on the day of judgment . . . We will be rewarded if our building is left standing"* (1 Corinthians 3:12, 14 CEV).

- *God's truth is the only foundation that will last.* The Bible tells us that *"the sound, wholesome teachings of the Lord Jesus Christ . . . are the foundation for a godly life"* (1 Timothy 6:3 NLT), and that *"God's truth stands firm like a foundation stone . . . "* (2 Timothy 2:19 NLT).

Jesus concluded his Sermon on the Mount with a story illustrating this important truth. Two houses were built on different foundations. The house built on sand was destroyed when rain, floods, and wind swept it away. But the house built on the foundation of solid rock remained firm. He concluded, *"Therefore everyone who hears these words of mine and puts them into practice is like a wise man who built his house on the rock"* (Matthew 7:24 NIV). *The Message* paraphrase of this verse shows how important this is: *"These words I speak to you are not incidental additions to your life . . . They are foundational words, words to build a life on."*

I cannot recommend this curriculum more highly to you. It has changed our church, our staff, and thousands of lives. For too long, too many have thought of theology as something that doesn't relate to our everyday lives, but *Foundations* explodes that mold. This study makes it clear that the foundation of what we do and say in each day of our lives is what we believe. I am thrilled that this in-depth, life-changing curriculum is now being made available for everyone to use.

— Rick Warren, author of *The Purpose Driven® Life*

PREFACE

Get ready for a radical statement, a pronouncement sure to make you wonder if we've lost our grip on reality: *There is nothing more exciting than doctrine!*

Track with us for a second on this. Doctrine is the study of what God has to say. What God has to say is always the truth. The truth gives me the right perspective on myself and on the world around me. The right perspective results in decisions of faith and experiences of joy. *That is exciting!*

The objective of *Foundations* is to present the basic truths of the Christian faith in a simple, systematic, and life-changing way—in other words, to teach doctrine. The question is, why? In a world in which people's lives are filled with crying needs, why teach doctrine? Because biblical doctrine has the answer to many of those crying needs! Please don't see this as a clash between needs-oriented and doctrine-oriented teaching. The truth is we need both. We all need to learn how to deal with worry in our lives. One of the keys to dealing with worry is an understanding of the biblical doctrine of the hope of heaven. Couples need to know what the Bible says about how to have a better marriage. They also need a deeper understanding of the doctrine of the Fatherhood of God, giving the assurance of God's love upon which all healthy relationships are built. Parents need to understand the Bible's practical insights for raising kids. They also need an understanding of the sovereignty of God, a certainty of the fact that God is in control, that will carry them through the inevitable ups and downs of being a parent. Doctrinal truth meets our deepest needs.

Welcome to a study that will have a lifelong impact on the way that you look at everything around you and above you and within you. Helping you develop a "Christian worldview" is our goal as the writers of this study. A Christian worldview is the ability to see everything through the filter of God's truth. The time you dedicate to this study will lay a foundation for new perspectives that will have tremendous benefits for the rest of your life. This study will help you:

- Lessen the stress in everyday life

- See the real potential for growth the Lord has given you

- Increase your sense of security in an often troubling world

- Find new tools for helping others (your friends, your family, your children) find the right perspective on life

- Fall more deeply in love with the Lord

Throughout this study you'll see four types of sidebar sections designed to help you connect with the truths God tells us about himself, ourselves, and this world.

- *A Closer Look:* We'll take time to expand on a truth or look at it from a different perspective.

- *A Fresh Word:* One aspect of doctrine that makes people nervous is the "big words." Throughout this study we'll take a fresh look at these words, words like *omnipotent* and *sovereign.*

- *Key Personal Perspective:* The truth of doctrine always has a profound impact on our lives. In this section we'll focus on that personal impact.

- *Living on Purpose:* James 1:22 (NCV) says, *"Do what God's teaching says; when you only listen and do nothing, you are fooling yourselves."* In his book, *The Purpose Driven Life,* Rick Warren identifies God's five purposes for our lives. They are worship, fellowship, discipleship, ministry, and evangelism. We will focus on one or two of these five purposes in each lesson, and discuss how it relates to the subject of the study. This section is very important, so please be sure to leave time for it.

Here is a brief explanation of the other features of this study guide.

Looking Ahead/Catching Up: You will open each meeting with an opportunity for everyone to check in with each other about how you are doing with the weekly assignments. Accountability is a key to success in this study!

Key Verse: Each week you will find a key verse or Scripture passage for your group to read together. If someone in the group has a different translation, ask them to read it aloud so the group can get a bigger picture of the meaning of the passage.

Video Lesson: There is a video lesson segment for the group to watch together each week. Take notes in the lesson outlines as you watch the video, and be sure to refer back to these notes during your discussion time.

Discovery Questions: Each video segment is complemented by questions for group discussion. Please don't feel pressured to discuss every single question. The material in this study is meant to be your servant, not your master, so there is no reason to rush through the answers. Give everyone ample opportunity to share their thoughts. If you don't get through all of the discovery questions, that's okay.

Prayer Direction: At the end of each session you will find suggestions for your group prayer time. Praying together is one of the greatest privileges of small group life. Please don't take it for granted.

Get ready for God to do incredible things in your life as you begin the adventure of learning more deeply about the most exciting message in the world: the truth about God!

— Tom Holladay and Kay Warren

HOW TO USE THIS VIDEO CURRICULUM

Here is a brief explanation of the features on your small group DVD. These features include a *Group Lifter,* four *Video Teaching Sessions* by Tom Holladay and Kay Warren, and a short video, *How to Become a Follower of Jesus Christ,* by Rick Warren. Here's how they work:

The *Group Lifter* is a brief video introduction by Tom Holladay giving you a sense of the objectives and purpose of this *Foundations* study on salvation. Watch it together as a group at the beginning of your first session.

The *Video Teaching Sessions* provide you with the teaching for each week of the study. Watch these features with your group. After watching the video teaching session, continue in your study by working through the discussion questions and activities in the study guide.

Nothing is more important than the decision you make to accept Jesus Christ as your Lord and Savior. Kay Warren presents two opportunities during this study to pray a prayer of salvation—at the end of Session Two and at the beginning of Session Four. We have also included a short video presentation, *How to Become a Follower of Jesus Christ,* that you can select at the end of either of those sessions or from the Main Menu on the DVD for viewing at any time. In this video segment, Rick Warren explains the importance of having Christ as the Savior of your life and how you can become part of the family of God.

Follow these simple steps for a successful small group session:

1. Hosts: Watch the video session and write down your answers to the discussion questions in the study guide before your group arrives.

2. Group: Open your group meeting by using the "Looking Ahead" or "Catching Up" section of your lesson.

3. Group: Watch the video teaching lesson and follow along in the outlines in the study guide.

4. Group: Complete the rest of the discussion materials for each session in the study guide.

It's just that simple. Have a great study together!

1

MAN'S PROBLEM,
GOD'S PROVISION

LOOKING AHEAD

1. What do you hope to get out of this small group study?

2. Share a time in your life when the word "rescue" took on real meaning for you or someone you know. What were the circumstances of that rescue? How did it impact you personally?

Key Verse

For it is by grace you have been saved, through faith—
and this not from yourselves, it is the gift of God.

Ephesians 2:8 (NIV)

BIBLE TEACHING
Watch the video lesson now and take notes in your outline on pages 3–5.

The Problem: Man's Need for Salvation

The major theme of the Bible is God's eternal plan to rescue us from our sin through Jesus' birth, his death on the cross, and his resurrection. God knew from the beginning that his creation would need a Savior, so he set in motion all that would be necessary to accomplish the salvation of his children.

To understand man's need for salvation we must look at two things: the nature of God and the nature of man.

The nature of God

We underestimate our need for a Savior because we underestimate who God is.

- God is _____

> *For this is what the high and lofty One says—he who lives forever, whose name is holy: "I live in a high and holy place, but also with him who is contrite and lowly in spirit, to revive the spirit of the lowly and to revive the heart of the contrite."* (Isaiah 57:15 NIV)

> *Exalt the LORD our God and worship at his holy mountain, for the LORD our God is holy* (Psalm 99:9 NIV)

God cannot tolerate anything that is evil.

- God is _____ and _____

Holiness has more to do with God's character.

Righteousness and justice have to do with God's dealings with mankind in relation to his character.

> *The LORD is gracious and righteous; our God is full of compassion.* (Psalm 116:5 NIV)

> *The Lord is fair in everything he does and full of kindness.* (Psalm 145:17 LB)

The nature of man

- Our nature: _____ (Genesis 2:17; Genesis 3)
- Our choice: _____ (Romans 3:10–18)
- Our condition: _____ (Luke 19:10)

A CLOSER LOOK

What Are the Consequences of Sin and Lostness?

- Sentenced to physical and spiritual death (Genesis 3:19; John 3:18; Romans 6:23)
- Separated from God (Ephesians 2:12)
- Dominated and controlled by sin (Ephesians 2:1–3; Romans 6:6)
- Spiritual blindness (2 Corinthians 4:3–4)
- Without understanding (Romans 3:11)
- Enemies of Christ (Matthew 12:30)
- Objects of God's wrath (Ephesians 2:3)
- Considered children of the Devil (John 8:44)

The Bible portrays mankind's lostness as the most pitiful condition imaginable. Not only is our life on earth wasted as we live for self and selfish desires but the consequence is eternal separation from God (Romans 6:23; Luke 13:3; Matthew 25:46).

The Provision: God's Solution to Sin

[25]God presented him as a sacrifice of atonement, through faith in his blood. He did this to demonstrate his justice, because in his forbearance he had left the sins committed beforehand unpunished—[26]he did it to demonstrate his justice at the present time, so as to be just and the one who justifies those who have faith in Jesus. (Romans 3:25–26 NIV)

Three central truths about salvation:

1. Salvation is not by works but by_____ .

   [8]For it is by grace you have been saved, through faith—and this not from yourselves, it is the gift of God—[9]not by works, so that no one can boast. (Ephesians 2:8–9 NIV)

2. Salvation is not initiated by us, but by_____ .

   [6]When we were unable to help ourselves, at the moment of our need, Christ died for us, although we were living against God. [7]Very few people will die to save the life of someone else. Although perhaps for a good person someone might possibly die. [8]But God shows his great love for us in this way: Christ died for us while we were still sinners. (Romans 5:6–8 NCV)

3. Salvation is not an afterthought with God; it is his _____ .

   [18b]You were bought . . . [19]with the precious blood of Christ, who was like a pure and perfect lamb. [20]Christ was chosen before the world was made, but he was shown to the world in these last times for your sake. (1 Peter 1:18b–20 NCV)

   It is God who saved us and chose us to live a holy life. He did this not because we deserved it, but because that was his plan long before the world began—to show his love and kindness to us through Christ Jesus. (1 Timothy 1:9 NLT)

DISCOVERY QUESTIONS

1. What have you heard in this session about the nature of God and the nature of man—God's holiness and man's unholiness? How has what you've heard enhanced your understanding of God's provision for us?

2. Some people, before coming to Christ, have a greater sense of being lost than others. Why do you think this is true? What causes one person to realize their lostness more clearly than another person?

3. What simply amazes you about God's salvation?

4. What impact do you want the understanding of God's love and provision to make in your life?

Once we understand God's love for us, including the lengths to which he has gone to provide for our salvation, we begin to feel a growing sense of urgency for the people around us who have not yet heard this good news.

Did You Get It? How has this week's study helped you see our deep need for salvation?

Share with Someone: Think of a person you can encourage with the truth you learned in this session. Write their name in the space below and pray for God to provide that opportunity this week.

LIVING ON PURPOSE

Evangelism

Ask God to help you sense the aloneness or emptiness of someone around you this week. How might he want you to come alongside that person and help them to see God's solution for their pain?

PRAYER DIRECTION

Spend a few minutes in prayer praising God for his holiness, righteousness, and justice. Thank him for your salvation. In short, one-sentence prayers, express your thankfulness for the characteristics of God we discussed in this session.

2

Session two

PICTURES OF SALVATION

CATCHING UP

1. Who did you share last week's truth with?

2. What did you learn about God's heart for the lost as a result of last week's "Living on Purpose" activity?

3. Did thoughts about God's provision of salvation encourage you in your daily life this last week? Briefly share a few insights.

Key Verse

For Christ died for sins once for all,
the righteous for the unrighteous, to bring you to God.

1 Peter 3:18a (NIV)

PICTURES of SALVATION

BIBLE TEACHING
Watch the video lesson now and take notes in your outline on pages 11–15.

Seven Descriptions of Salvation

One: _____—Jesus died in my place.

> *For Christ died for sins once for all, the righteous for the unrighteous, to bring you to God. He was put to death in the body but made alive by the Spirit.* (1 Peter 3:18 NIV)

What does it mean when we say Jesus became our substitute?

- He was made sin for me (2 Corinthians 5:21).
- He bore my sin in his body on the cross (1 Peter 2:24).
- He suffered once to bear the sins of others (Hebrews 9:28).
- He was tortured for others' sin (Isaiah 53:4–6).
- He was made a curse for me (Galatians 3:13).

> *I have been crucified with Christ and I no longer live, but Christ lives in me. The life I live in the body, I live by faith in the Son of God, who loved me and gave himself for me.* (Galatians 2:20 NIV)

Two: _____—Jesus made me right with God.

> *Through him everyone who believes is justified from everything you could not be justified from by the law of Moses.* (Acts 13:39 NIV)

He was delivered over to death for our sins and was raised to life for our justification. (Romans 4:25 NIV)

Three: _____—Jesus made peace with God possible.

God was in Christ, making peace between the world and himself . . . God did not hold the world guilty of its sins. And he gave us this message of peace. (2 Corinthians 5:19 NCV)

Jesus is the bridge between God and man.

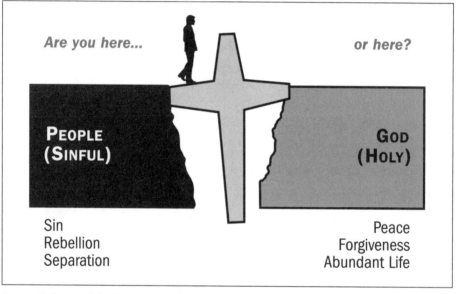

Are you here...   or here?

**PEOPLE
(SINFUL)**

**GOD
(HOLY)**

Sin
Rebellion
Separation

Peace
Forgiveness
Abundant Life

Source: Bridge to Life by the Navigators (Colorado Springs: NavPress, 1969.)

Four: _____—Jesus made me a part of God's family.

He predestined us to be adopted as his sons through Jesus Christ, in accordance with his pleasure and will.
(Ephesians 1:5 NIV)

You are God's child by his choice!

Five: _____—Jesus purchased my salvation with his blood.

A FRESH WORD

Redemption

The Greek word for *redemption* refers to slaves being purchased in the marketplace. In the spiritual sense, all of us were slaves to sin until Jesus purchased us out of the slave market and set us free from sin's bondage. Because he bought and paid for us with his blood, we now belong exclusively to him.

---

[13]*For he has rescued us from the dominion of darkness and brought us into the kingdom of the Son he loves,* [14]*in whom we have redemption, the forgiveness of sins.*
(Colossians 1:13–14 NIV)

[18]*God paid a ransom to save you from the impossible road to heaven which your fathers tried to take, and the ransom he paid was not mere gold or silver as you very well know.* [19]*But he paid for you with the precious lifeblood of Christ, the sinless, spotless Lamb of God.* (1 Peter 1:18–19 LB)

Six: _____—Jesus satisfied God's justice.

A FRESH WORD

Propitiation

To *propitiate* is to bring satisfaction or to fulfill a demand or requirement. In heathen circles it was a word that meant "to appease the gods." The biblical sense of the word speaks of that which satisfies the justice of God so that mercy is given.

The picture of propitiation in the Old Testament is the_____ .

The mercy seat, or atonement cover, is the cover of the ark of the covenant in first the tabernacle and later the temple. This is the place where the high priest sprinkled the blood of sacrifice as an offering for the sins of the people.

Jesus became all three of these for us. He is the high priest who makes the offering for our sins. He is also the sacrifice who shed his blood for our sin, and he himself is the place of mercy where we find forgiveness for our sin.

> He is the atoning sacrifice for our sins, and not only for ours but also for the sins of the whole world. (1 John 2:2 NIV)

Seven: _____—Jesus sent my sins away from me.

> In him we have redemption through his blood, the forgiveness of sins, in accordance with the riches of God's grace. (Ephesians 1:7 NIV)

> As far as the east is from the west, so far has he removed our transgressions from us. (Psalm 103:12 NIV)

> You will throw away all our sins into the deepest part of the sea. (Micah 7:19 NCV)

Three aspects of salvation: past, present, and future

- In the past: I was saved from the _____ of sin (justification)

- In the present: I am being saved from the _____ of sin (sanctification)

- In the future: I will be saved from the _____ of sin (glorification)

This means that while Jesus' death accomplished all that God intended it to—Jesus said, "It is finished"—we have not experienced all there is to experience of salvation. There is more to look forward to!

KEY PERSONAL PERSPECTIVE

What do I need to know to be saved?

Does someone have to be able to understand all the truths we've discussed today to be saved? No.

To be saved you need to know only three truths:

1. I am a sinner.

2. Jesus died in my place.

3. If I ask God to forgive me for rebelling against him and I trust in Jesus as my Lord, he will save me.

No one can say these three truths are difficult to understand. The truth of our salvation is simple enough for a child to understand, yet deep enough to study the rest of your life and never fully comprehend.

The bottom-line question: Have you accepted God's gift of forgiveness for your sin, paid for by Jesus' death on the cross?

Prayer of Salvation

Father, I admit to you that I am a sinner. I thank you that Jesus died in my place. And I ask you now to forgive me for rebelling against you, and I trust in Jesus as the Lord, the manager of my life. Father, I trust you to give me the gift of salvation.

DISCOVERY QUESTIONS

1. As each of the descriptions or pictures of salvation was shared, which had the most emotional impact for you? Which would you like to understand more clearly?

2. The truth of justification, that Jesus makes us right before God, is difficult for many to understand. Why do we struggle to see ourselves as not guilty before God? What has helped increase your faith in God's promise that we are justified?

3. What has encouraged you to focus daily on the truth that salvation is not the result of anything we did, but instead is the result of God's grace? What are some ways you might slip into taking credit for your salvation, and how can you make certain the thanks goes to God alone?

4. Our salvation has three aspects: past, present, and future. Choose one of the three and share with the group one way this characteristic of salvation is particularly meaningful to you today.

> ## "HOW TO BECOME A FOLLOWER OF JESUS CHRIST"
>
> Have you ever surrendered your life to Jesus Christ? Take a few minutes with your group to watch a brief video by Pastor Rick Warren on how to become part of the family of God. It is included on the Main Menu of this DVD.

Did You Get It? How has this week's study, discussing the pictures God gives us of salvation, helped you to better understand salvation?

Share with Someone: Think of a person you can encourage with the truth you learned in this session. Write their name in the space below and pray for God to provide that opportunity this week.

LIVING ON PURPOSE
Evangelism

Which of the seven descriptions of salvation we studied in this session could you use right now to help someone better understand how to become a follower of Jesus Christ?

In the Small Group Resources section on page 51 we have included a tool, "How to Establish a 'Spiritual Base' for Your Life," to help you share the truth of Christ with others. Take some time in your session today to role-play the use of this card. This will help each of you feel more comfortable using this tool in the future as you share the gospel with others.

- Pair up with someone in your group to walk through the Base Card on pages 51–52. The card uses the acrostic BASE. Read aloud each statement and the accompanying verse.

- When you have completed each step and your partner has expressed his/her desire to take these steps, pray the prayer at the bottom of the card with him/her.

- Practice using the card with a family member at home this week. Continued practice will help you become more and more confident sharing these truths when opportunities arise.

Remember that because each person in your life is uniquely created by God, his manner of reaching them through you is likely to be different for each individual.

PRAYER DIRECTION

Take some time as a group to talk about your specific prayer requests and to pray for one another. Thank God for each of the wonderful pictures of salvation he provided in his Word and for what they mean to you personally.

Are there any answers to report to last week's prayers? If so, celebrate these responses from God.

3

Session three

ASSURANCE OF SALVATION

CATCHING UP

1. Who did you share last week's truth with?

2. What did you learn about sharing God's plan of salvation during last week's "Living on Purpose" activity?

3. As a child, what was your greatest fear? How did you learn to deal with that fear? Did anyone or anything assist you in relating to or overcoming that fear? Briefly share your memories.

Key Verse

*"My sheep listen to my voice; I know them, and they follow me.
I give them eternal life, and they never perish;
no one can snatch them out of my hand."*

John 10:27–28 (NIV)

BIBLE TEACHING
Watch the video lesson now and take notes in your outline on pages 21–24.

Why Do So Many People Lack the Assurance of Salvation?

1. Because they cannot pinpoint a _____ when they received Christ.

2. Because they question the _____ of the way they expressed faith in Christ.

3. Because of _____ they commit after salvation.

There is a difference between the personal assurance of my salvation and the promised security of my salvation. While I may or may not have a *feeling* of assurance, security is a *fact* based on the promise of God.

The Promised Security of Salvation

Each member of the Trinity plays a part in our security as believers.

The sovereign decision of the Father

- God has declared us _____ in his sight

  "For God so loved the world that he gave his one and only Son, that whoever believes in him shall not perish but have eternal life." (John 3:16 NIV)

- God is at peace with _____

Therefore, since we have been made right in God's sight by faith, we have peace with God because of what Jesus Christ our Lord has done for us. (Romans 5:1 NLT)

- God has determined that nothing can ever _____ me from his love

  [38]For I am convinced that neither death nor life, neither angels nor demons, neither the present nor the future, nor any powers, [39]neither height nor depth, nor anything else in all creation, will be able to separate us from the love of God that is in Christ Jesus our Lord. (Romans 8:38–39 NIV)

The high-priestly work of Jesus Christ

A CLOSER LOOK

Jesus As Our High Priest

In the Old Testament sacrificial system, the high priest was the highest spiritual leader. He alone got to enter the Holy of Holies and put blood on the mercy seat once a year on the Day of Atonement. Jesus is our High Priest. When Jesus died on the cross, he was both the ultimate sacrifice and the ultimate sacrificer. He lives forever to do the work of a high priest—to be our intercessor and our mediator.

- Jesus lives to make _____ for me

  Therefore he is able to save completely those who come to God through him, because he always lives to intercede for them. (Hebrews 7:25 NIV)

- Jesus lives to _____ for me

¹My dear children, I write this to you so that you will not sin. But if anybody does sin, we have one who speaks to the Father in our defense—Jesus Christ, the Righteous One. ²He is the atoning sacrifice for our sins, and not only for ours but also for the sins of the whole world. (1 John 2:1-2 NIV)

- Jesus is _____ to me even when I am not faithful to him

¹¹This teaching is true: If we died with him, we will also live with him. ¹²If we accept suffering, we will also rule with him. If we refuse to accept him, he will refuse to accept us. ¹³If we are not faithful, he will still be faithful, because he cannot be false to himself. (2 Timothy 2:11-13 NCV)

Let us hold unswervingly to the hope we profess, for he who promised is faithful. (Hebrews 10:23 NIV)

The sealing power of the Holy Spirit

In our study of the Holy Spirit, we saw that at the moment of salvation, the Holy Spirit performs several works on our behalf that secure our salvation forever.

- The Holy Spirit regenerates me (gives me new birth)
- The Holy Spirit baptizes me
- The Holy Spirit abides in me as a gift from God
- The Holy Spirit seals me

And you were also included in Christ when you heard the word of truth, the gospel of your salvation. Having believed, you were marked in him with a seal, the promised Holy Spirit. (Ephesians 1:13 NIV)

We can be certain of the security of our salvation because in the past, Christ made peace with God for each of us. Today, Jesus lives to make intercession for me, and the Holy Spirit guarantees that my future is full of glory. It is God's work that makes my salvation secure—I can do nothing to make him stop loving me or stop being faithful to his own promises.

> [27]"My sheep listen to my voice; I know them, and they follow me. [28]I give them eternal life, and they shall never perish; no one can snatch them out of my hand. [29]My Father, who has given them to me, is greater than all; no one can snatch them out of my Father's hand." (John 10:27–29 NIV)

DISCOVERY QUESTIONS

1. Look back at the three reasons why people lack assurance of salvation. Which one do you think people struggle with the most? Has one of these been a struggle for you?

2. What is the difference between basing my sense of security in salvation on my faithfulness to God as opposed to basing it on his faithfulness to me? How does the truth of God's faithfulness impact our attitudes, motivations, and actions as believers?

3. How does the "high-priestly work of Jesus" help you picture the importance of his role in your everyday life?

Did You Get It? How has this week's study helped you see the assurance of God's promise of salvation?

Share with Someone: Think of a person you can encourage with the truth you learned in this session. Write their name in the space below and pray for God to provide that opportunity this week.

LIVING ON PURPOSE

Discipleship

During your quiet time this next week, read John's gospel account of the price Jesus paid for our salvation. Read John 14–20, one chapter a day over the next seven days.

PRAYER DIRECTION

Pray together for those you know who do not yet know Christ. Make a list of their names as you pray to remind you to 1) pray for them more often, and 2) rejoice when your prayers are answered as they make a commitment to Jesus.

Preparation for Next Time: For next week's "Living on Purpose" activity, you will share the Lord's Supper together as a group. The Lord's Supper is an expression of participating in the life and death of Jesus Christ. When we share this experience together we worship our Lord for coming, dying, and providing the opportunity for eternal life. Take a few moments now to plan this time of communion. Turn to page 53 in the Small Group Resources section for instructions.

Session four

4

PERSONAL SECURITY

CATCHING UP

1. What did you learn about your salvation from reading the Gospel according to John during last week's "Living on Purpose" activity?

2. Describe a time when the sense of security in your relationship with God was greatest. Why did you feel so secure at that time? What, if anything, changed that sense of security?

Key Verse

Let us draw near to God with a sincere heart in full assurance of faith . . .

Hebrews 10:22a (NIV)

BIBLE TEACHING
Watch the video lesson now and take notes in your outline on pages 29–33.

The Personal Assurance of Your Salvation

How do you handle _____ *about your salvation?*

Whenever a person is not sure if they are saved, there are several possibilities:

- They may not be saved
- They may be disobeying God
- They may be experiencing temptation from Satan to doubt

Three kinds of security:

- False security
- Conditional security
- Eternal security

What if you can't _____ *you became a Christian?*

Some people can't remember exactly when their moment of "spiritual birth" was and it bothers them. If you've doubted your salvation and can't remember when it happened, take a moment to pray the following prayer.

Prayer for Assurance

Jesus, I know I made this commitment before, but not being able to remember exactly when has caused me some real doubts. So right here and right now, on (say the date) I nail down in my heart the fact that my life is given to you. I trust in you and you alone to forgive the wrong things that I've done. I ask you to be the Lord—the leader and manager—of my life. Amen.

If you aren't sure that you are a Christian, make sure right now. Ask Jesus to forgive you of your sins and to come into your heart and life.

And when Satan tries to hassle you and cause you to wonder about whether you really are a believer, you can point to this day and remember that you did ask Jesus to be your Savior.

What happens to my relationship to God when I sin?

- When a Christian sins, _____ with God is
  broken, but the _____ remains intact.

God has said that we have been adopted into his family with all the rights and privileges of his Son, Jesus. He will never disown Jesus; he'll never disown us. But sin in our lives must be dealt with. Look at these diagrams to follow the process of what happens when a Christian sins.

SIN BARRIERS BEFORE SALVATION

Barriers on God's side		Barriers on man's side	
God	1. God's justice demands punishment of the guilty. 2. God's holiness demands rejection of the unholy. 3. God's perfection demands devaluation of the imperfect.	1. Man's knowledge of his guilt brings fear of punishment. 2. Man's knowledge of his lack of holiness brings fear of rejection. 3. Man's knowledge of his imperfection brings loss of self-esteem.	Man

SIN BARRIERS AFTER SALVATION WHEN WE FORGET THAT GOD TOTALLY ACCEPTS US

Barriers on God's side		Barriers on man's side	
God	Totally removed by Christ's death	Expectancy of punishment, rejections, and loss of self-esteem all resulting from our early experiences with punishment.	Man

SIN BARRIERS AFTER SALVATION WHEN WE HAVE FULLY APPLIED THE RESULTS OF CHRIST'S ATONEMENT

Barriers on God's side		Barriers on man's side	
God	Totally removed by Christ's death	Totally removed by the knowledge of God's total acceptance and forgiveness and by the realization that God doesn't motivate by threats of punishment, rejection, and lowered self-esteem.	Man

EFFECTS OF SIN ON THE CHRISTIAN

What Sin Doesn't Do	What Sin Does Do
1. Bring punishment from God. 2. Make God angry with us. 3. Cause God to reject us, even temporarily. 4. Make us worthless or valueless to God. 5. Cause God to make us feel guilty.	1. Brings loving correction and discipline from God. 2. Interferes with our best personal adjustment, harms us, and eventually makes us unhappy. 3. Decreases our effectiveness in the world. 4. Damages the lives of others—especially those closest to us. 5. Brings loss of rewards in heaven. 6. Brings conviction from God.

Diagrams and chart adapted from Bruce Narramore and Bill Counts, *Freedom from Guilt* (Santa Ana, Calif.: Vision House, 1974), 83–85, 93.

Are there any _____ that you are a Christian?

While God alone can see into the hearts of individuals and determine who has honestly committed themselves to him, he has told us in his Word that there are some evidences by which we are to judge ourselves, not others.

Proofs of Salvation:

- The _____ that God is our heavenly Father
- A new reliance on _____
- A new ability to understand _____
- A new sense of the seriousness of _____
- A new _____ for lost people
- A new love for _____

KEY PERSONAL PERSPECTIVE

Why should God allow me into his heaven?

Question: Why should God allow me into his heaven?

Only Answer: Because I've _____ in Christ's work on the cross.

Not . . .

      because I'm a good person.

      because I believe in God.

      because I go to church.

If you can answer this question correctly, you can relinquish your doubts and fears about the security of your salvation. Begin to live in the freedom that comes from knowing your salvation is secure.

Let us go right in to God himself, with true hearts fully trusting him to receive us because we have been sprinkled with Christ's blood to make us clean . . . (Hebrews 10:22 LB)

DISCOVERY QUESTIONS

1. Look back over the outline on pages 29–33. What have we covered in this session that has had the greatest impact on your confidence in your standing before God?

2. What would be your response if a friend were to say the following to you? "I've been attending church and praying and trying to read the Bible for years, but lately I've been feeling like I'm not really a Christian."

3. If our salvation is eternally secure, where does the daily motivation to grow spiritually come from? Consider the following reasons and choose the one most significant to you. Share with the group why you chose the one you did.

Grace

> *⁸For it is by grace you have been saved, through faith—and this not from yourselves, it is the gift of God—⁹not by works, so that no one can boast. ¹⁰For we are God's workmanship, created in Christ Jesus to do good works, which God prepared in advance for us to do.* (Ephesians 2:8–10 NIV)

Eternal rewards

> *Whatever you do, work at it with all your heart, as working for the Lord, not for men.* (Colossians 3:23 NIV)

Pleasing God

> *So we make it our goal to please him, whether we are at home in the body or away from it.* (2 Corinthians 5:9 NIV)

4. Over the past two weeks we have addressed the assurance and security of our salvation, but sometimes we don't "feel" secure and doubts remain. Is anyone in your group still struggling with doubts about his/her standing before God? If so, share your doubts with the group. Has anyone else ever experienced this doubt? How did you deal with it? As a group, commit to helping those who have doubts resolve them.

"HOW TO BECOME A FOLLOWER OF JESUS CHRIST"

Have you ever surrendered your life to Jesus Christ? Take a few minutes with your group to watch a brief video by Pastor Rick Warren on how to become part of the family of God. It is included on the Main Menu of this DVD.

Did You Get It? How has this week's study helped you deal with any doubts you may have had about your salvation?

Share with Someone: Think of a person you can encourage with the truth you learned in this session. Write their name in the space below and pray for God to provide that opportunity this week.

LIVING ON PURPOSE
Worship
Share the Lord's Supper together. Steps for serving communion are included in the Small Group Resources section on page 53.

PRAYER DIRECTION

Take some time as a group to talk about your specific prayer requests and to pray for one another.

SmalL Group Resources

HELPS FOR HOSTS

Top Ten Ideas for New Hosts

Congratulations! As the host of your small group, you have responded to the call to help shepherd Jesus' flock. Few other tasks in the family of God surpass the contribution you will be making.

As you prepare to facilitate your group, whether it is one session or the entire series, here are a few thoughts to keep in mind. We encourage you to read and review these tips with each new discussion host before he or she leads.

Remember you are not alone. God knows everything about you, and he knew you would be asked to facilitate your group. Even though you may not feel ready, this is common for all good hosts. God promises, *"I will never leave you; I will never abandon you"* (Hebrews 13:5 TEV). Whether you are facilitating for one evening, several weeks, or a lifetime, you will be blessed as you serve.

1. **Don't try to do it alone.** Pray right now for God to help you build a healthy team. If you can enlist a cohost to help you shepherd the group, you will find your experience much richer. This is your chance to involve as many people as you can in building a healthy group. All you have to do is ask people to help. You'll be surprised at the response.

2. **Be friendly and be yourself.** God wants to use your unique gifts and temperament. Be sure to greet people at the door with a big smile . . . this can set the mood for the whole gathering. Remember, they are taking as big a step to show up at your house as you are to lead this group! Don't try to do things exactly like another host; do them in a way that fits you. Admit when you don't have an answer and apologize when you make a mistake. Your group will love you for it and you'll sleep better at night.

3. **Prepare for your meeting ahead of time.** Review the session and write down your responses to each question. Pay special attention to exercises that ask group members to do something other than engage in discussion. These exercises will help your group live what the Bible teaches, not just talk about it. Be sure you understand how an exercise works. If the exercise employs one of the items in the Small Group Resources section (such as the Group Guidelines), be sure to look over that item so you'll know how it works.

4. **Pray for your group members by name.** Before you begin your session, take a few moments and pray for each member by name. You may want to review the prayer list at least once a week. Ask God to use your time together to touch the heart of every person in your group. Expect God to lead you to whomever he wants you to encourage or challenge in a special way. If you listen, God will surely lead.

5. **When you ask a question, be patient.** Someone will eventually respond. Sometimes people need a moment or two of silence to think about the question. If silence doesn't bother you, it won't bother anyone else. After someone responds, affirm the response with a simple "thanks" or "great answer." Then ask, "How about somebody else?" or "Would someone who hasn't shared like to add anything?" Be sensitive to new people or reluctant members who aren't ready to say, pray, or do anything. If you give them a safe setting, they will blossom over time. If someone in your group is a "wallflower" who sits silently through every session, consider talking to them privately and encouraging them to participate. Let them know how important they are to you—that they are loved and appreciated—and that the group would value their input. Remember, still water often runs deep.

6. **Provide transitions between questions.** Ask if anyone would like to read the paragraph or Bible passage. Don't call on anyone, but ask for a volunteer, and then be patient until someone begins. Be sure to thank the person who reads aloud.

7. **Break into smaller groups occasionally.** With a greater opportunity to talk in a small circle, people will connect more with the study, apply more quickly what they're learning, and ultimately get more out of their small group experience. A small circle also encourages a quiet person to participate and tends to minimize the effects of a more vocal or dominant member.

8. **Small circles are also helpful during prayer time.** People who are unaccustomed to praying aloud will feel more comfortable trying it with just two or three others. Also, prayer requests won't take as much time, so circles will have more time to actually pray. When you gather back with the whole group, you can have one person from each circle briefly update everyone on the prayer requests from their subgroups. The other great aspect of subgrouping is that it fosters leadership development. As you ask people in the group to facilitate discussion or to lead a prayer circle, it gives them a small leadership step that can build their confidence.

9. **Rotate facilitators occasionally.** You may be perfectly capable of hosting each time, but you will help others grow in their faith and gifts if you give them opportunities to host the group.

10. **One final challenge (for new or first-time hosts).** Before your first opportunity to lead, look up each of the six passages that follow. Read each one as a devotional exercise to help prepare you with a shepherd's heart. Trust us on this one. If you do this, you will be more than ready for your first meeting.

Matthew 9:36–38 (NIV)
36When Jesus saw the crowds, he had compassion on them, because they were harassed and helpless, like sheep without a shepherd. 37Then he said to his disciples, "The harvest is plentiful but the workers are few. 38Ask the Lord of the harvest, therefore, to send out workers into his harvest field."

John 10:14–15 (NIV)
14I am the good shepherd; I know my sheep and my sheep know me—15just as the Father knows me and I know the Father—and I lay down my life for the sheep.

1 Peter 5:2–4 (NIV)

²Be shepherds of God's flock that is under your care, serving as overseers—not because you must, but because you are willing, as God wants you to be; ³not greedy for money, but eager to serve; not lording it over those entrusted to you, but being examples to the flock. ⁴And when the Chief Shepherd appears, you will receive the crown of glory that will never fade away.

Philippians 2:1–5 (NIV)

¹If you have any encouragement from being united with Christ, if any comfort from his love, if any fellowship with the Spirit, if any tenderness and compassion, ²then make my joy complete by being like-minded, having the same love, being one in spirit and purpose. ³Do nothing out of selfish ambition or vain conceit, but in humility consider others better than yourselves. ⁴Each of you should look not only to your own interests, but also to the interests of others. ⁵Your attitude should be the same as that of Jesus Christ.

Hebrews 10:23–25 (NIV)

²³Let us hold unswervingly to the hope we profess, for he who promised is faithful. ²⁴And let us consider how we may spur one another on toward love and good deeds. ²⁵Let us not give up meeting together, as some are in the habit of doing, but let us encourage one another—and all the more as you see the Day approaching.

1 Thessalonians 2:7–8, 11–12 (NIV)

⁷. . . but we were gentle among you, like a mother caring for her little children. ⁸We loved you so much that we were delighted to share with you not only the gospel of God but our lives as well, because you had become so dear to us. . . . ¹¹For you know that we dealt with each of you as a father deals with his own children, ¹²encouraging, comforting and urging you to live lives worthy of God, who calls you into his kingdom and glory.

FREQUENTLY ASKED QUESTIONS

How long will this group meet?

This volume of *Foundations: Salvation* is four sessions long. We encourage your group to add a fifth session for a celebration. In your final session, each group member may decide if he or she desires to continue on for another study. At that time you may also want to do some informal evaluation, discuss your Group Guidelines, and decide which study you want to do next. We recommend you visit our website at **www.saddlebackresources.com** for more video-based small group studies.

Who is the host?

The host is the person who coordinates and facilitates your group meetings. In addition to a host, we encourage you to select one or more group members to lead your group discussions. Several other responsibilities can be rotated, including refreshments, prayer requests, worship, or keeping up with those who miss a meeting. Shared ownership in the group helps everybody grow.

Where do we find new group members?

Recruiting new members can be a challenge for groups, especially new groups with just a few people, or existing groups that lose a few people along the way. We encourage you to use the *Circles of Life* diagram on page 46 of this DVD study guide to brainstorm a list of people from your workplace, church, school, neighborhood, family, and so on. Then pray for the people on each member's list. Allow each member to invite several people from their list. Some groups fear that newcomers will interrupt the intimacy that members have built over time. However, groups that welcome newcomers generally gain strength with the infusion of new blood. Remember, the next person you add just might become a friend for eternity. Logistically, groups find different ways to add members. Some groups remain permanently open, while others choose to open periodically, such as at the beginning or end of a study. If your group becomes too large for easy, face-to-face conversations, you can subgroup, forming a second discussion group in another room.

How do we handle the child care needs in our group?

Child care needs must be handled very carefully. This is a sensitive issue. We suggest you seek creative solutions as a group. One common solution is to have the adults meet in the living room and share the cost of a babysitter (or two) who can be with the kids in another part of the house. Another popular option is to have one home for the kids (supervised, of course) and a second home (close by) for the adults. If desired, the adults could rotate the responsibility of providing a lesson for the kids. This last option is great with school-age kids and can be a huge blessing to families.

GROUP GUIDELINES

It's a good idea for every group to put words to their shared values, expectations, and commitments. Such guidelines will help you avoid unspoken agendas and unmet expectations. We recommend you discuss your guidelines during Session One in order to lay the foundation for a healthy group experience. Feel free to modify anything that does not work for your group.

We agree to the following values:

Clear Purpose
To grow healthy spiritual lives by building a healthy small group community

Group Attendance
To give priority to the group meeting (call if I am absent or late)

Safe Environment
To create a safe place where people can be heard and feel loved (no quick answers, snap judgments, or simple fixes)

Be Confidential
To keep anything that is shared strictly confidential and within the group

Conflict Resolution
To avoid gossip and to immediately resolve any concerns by following the principles of Matthew 18:15–17

Spiritual Health
To give group members permission to speak into my life and help me live a healthy, balanced spiritual life that is pleasing to God

Limit Our Freedom
To limit our freedom by not serving or consuming alcohol during small group meetings or events so as to avoid causing a weaker brother or sister to stumble (1 Corinthians 8:1–13; Romans 14:19–21)

Welcome Newcomers   To invite friends who might benefit from this study and warmly welcome newcomers

Building Relationships   To get to know the other members of the group and pray for them regularly

Other   _____

We have also discussed and agreed on the following items:

Child Care

_____

_____

Starting Time

_____

Ending Time

_____

If you haven't already done so, take a few minutes to fill out the *Small Group Calendar* on page 50.

CIRCLES OF LIFE—SMALL GROUP CONNECTIONS

Discover who you can connect in community

Use this chart to help carry out one of the values in the Group Guidelines to "Welcome Newcomers."

"Follow me, and I will make you fishers of men." (Matthew 4:19 KJV)

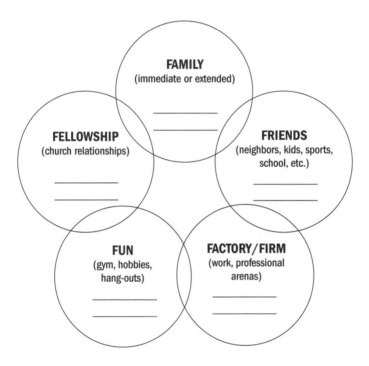

Follow this simple three-step process:

1. List 1–2 people in each circle.

2. Prayerfully select one person or couple from your list and tell your group about them.

3. Give them a call and invite them to your next meeting. Over 50 percent of those invited to a small group say, "Yes!"

SMALL GROUP PRAYER AND PRAISE REPORT

This is a place where you can write each other's requests for prayer. You can also make a note when God answers a prayer. Pray for each other's requests. If you're new to group prayer, it's okay to pray silently or to pray by using just one sentence: "God, please help

_____ to _____ ."

DATE	PERSON	PRAYER REQUEST	PRAISE REPORT

SMALL GROUP PRAYER AND PRAISE REPORT

DATE	PERSON	PRAYER REQUEST	PRAISE REPORT

SMALL GROUP PRAYER AND PRAISE REPORT

DATE	PERSON	PRAYER REQUEST	PRAISE REPORT

SMALL GROUP CALENDAR

Healthy groups share responsibilities and group ownership. It might take some time for this to develop. Shared ownership ensures that responsibility for the group doesn't fall to one person. Use the calendar to keep track of social events, mission projects, birthdays, or days off. Complete this calendar at your first or second meeting. Planning ahead will increase attendance and shared ownership.

DATE	LESSON	LOCATION	FACILITATOR	SNACK OR MEAL
5/4	Session 2	Chris and Andrea	Jim Brown	Phil and Karen

BASE CARD

THE LIFE WE'RE MEANT TO LIVE

How to Establish a "Spiritual BASE" for Your Life
(from the Bible)

Believe God made me to love me and to live for his purposes.

> *... everything got started in [God] and finds its purpose in him.* (Colossians 1:16b MSG)

> *Long before [God] laid down earth's foundations, he had us in mind, had settled on us as the focus of his love ...* (Ephesians 1:4 MSG)

Admit I've lived for myself, then accept God's free forgiveness which was paid for by Jesus.

> *We're all like sheep who've wandered off and gotten lost. We've all done our own thing, gone our own way. And GOD has piled all our sins, everything we've done wrong, on him (Jesus).* (Isaiah 53:6 MSG)

> *[Jesus] personally carried the load of our sins in his own body when he died on the cross so that we can be finished with sin and live a good life from now on ...* (1 Peter 2:24 LB)

> *Saving is all [God's] idea, and all his work. All we do is trust him enough to let him do it. It's God's gift from start to finish!* (Ephesians 2:8 MSG)

BASE CARD

Switch to living for God's purposes for my life.

> *... give yourselves to God ... and surrender your whole being to him to be used for righteous purposes.* (Romans 6:13b TEV)

Express my desire for Jesus to be the Lord (leader) of my life.

> *So you will be saved, if you honestly say, "Jesus is Lord," and if you believe with all your heart that God raised him from death.* (Romans 10:9 CEV)

> *It makes no difference who you are or where you're from—if you want God and are ready to do as he says, the door is open.* (Acts 10:35 MSG)

A simple prayer you can pray:

Dear God, I don't understand it all yet, but I believe you love me and made me for your purposes. I'm sorry that I've lived for myself instead of for you, and I ask for your forgiveness. Thank you for sending Jesus to pay for my sins. I want Jesus to be the Lord of my life. Please help me to learn to love you and trust you and live for your purposes. Amen.

SERVING THE LORD'S SUPPER

²³ . . . The Lord Jesus, on the night he was betrayed, took bread, ²⁴and when he had given thanks, he broke it and said, "This is my body, which is for you; do this in remembrance of me." ²⁵In the same way, after supper he took the cup, saying, "This cup is the new covenant in my blood; do this, whenever you drink it, in remembrance of me." ²⁶For whenever you eat this bread and drink this cup, you proclaim the Lord's death until he comes. (1 Corinthians 11:23–26 NIV)

Steps in Serving Communion

(Before serving communion in your small group, check with your pastor and church leadership to be sure that serving communion in a small group fits the practice and philosophy of your church.)

1. Open by sharing about God's love, forgiveness, grace, mercy, commitment, tenderheartedness, faithfulness, etc., out of your personal journey (connect with stories of those in the room).

2. Read the passage: *. . . The Lord Jesus, on the night he was betrayed, took bread, and when he had given thanks, he broke it and said, "This is my body, which is for you; do this in remembrance of me."* (vv. 23–24)

3. Pray and pass the bread around the circle (could be time for quiet reflection, singing a simple praise song, or listening to a worship tape).

4. When everyone has been served, remind him or her that this represents Jesus' body broken on their behalf. Simply state, "Jesus said, *'Do this in remembrance of me.'* Let us eat together," and eat the bread as a group.

5. Then read the rest of the passage: *In the same way, after supper he took the cup, saying, "This cup is the new covenant in my blood; do this, whenever you drink it, in remembrance of me."* (v. 25)

6. Pray and serve the cups, either by passing a small tray, serving them individually, or having members pick up a cup from the table.

7. When everyone has been served, remind them the juice represents Christ's blood shed for them, then simply state, "Take and drink in remembrance of him. Let us drink together."

8. Finish by singing a simple song, listening to a praise song, or having a time of prayer in thanks to God.

Several Practical Tips in Serving Communion

1. Be sensitive to timing in your meeting.

2. Break up pieces of cracker or soft bread on a small plate or tray. Don't use large servings of bread or juice.

3. Prepare all of the elements beforehand and bring these into the room when you are ready.

Communion passages: Matthew 26:26–29; Mark 14:22–25; Luke 22:14–20; 1 Corinthians 10:16–21, 11:17–34

ANSWER KEY

Session One: Man's Problem, God's Provision

- God is <u>holy</u>
- God is <u>righteous</u> and <u>just</u>

- Our nature: <u>we are sinful</u>
- Our choice: <u>we sin</u>
- Our condition: <u>we are lost</u>

1. Salvation is not by works but by <u>grace</u>.
2. Salvation is not initiated by us, but by <u>God</u>.
3. Salvation is not an afterthought with God; it is his <u>eternal plan</u>.

Session Two: Pictures of Salvation

One: <u>*Substitution*</u>*—Jesus died in my place.*

Two: <u>*Justification*</u>*—Jesus made me right with God.*

Three: <u>*Reconciliation*</u>*—Jesus made peace with God possible.*

Four: <u>*Adoption*</u>*—Jesus made me a part of God's family.*

Five: <u>*Redemption*</u>*—Jesus purchased my salvation with his blood.*

Six: <u>*Propitiation*</u>*—Jesus satisfied God's justice.*

   The picture of propitiation in the Old Testament is the mercy seat.

Seven: <u>*Forgiveness*</u>*—Jesus sent my sins away from me.*

- In the past: I was saved from the <u>penalty</u> of sin (justification)
- In the present: I am being saved from the <u>power</u> of sin (sanctification)
- In the future: I will be saved from the <u>presence</u> of sin (glorification)

Session Three: Assurance of Salvation

1. Because they cannot pinpoint a <u>specific time</u> when they received Christ.
2. Because they question the <u>correctness</u> of the way they expressed faith in Christ.
3. Because of <u>sins</u> they commit after salvation.

- God has declared us <u>"not guilty"</u> in his sight
- God is at peace with <u>me</u>
- God has determined that nothing can ever <u>separate</u> me from his love

- Jesus lives to make <u>intercession</u> for me
- Jesus lives to <u>mediate</u> for me
- Jesus is <u>faithful</u> to me even when I am not faithful to him

Session Four: Personal Security

How do you handle <u>doubts</u> about your salvation?

What if you can't <u>remember when</u> you became a Christian?

- When a Christian sins, <u>fellowship</u> with God is broken, but the <u>relationship</u> remains intact.

Are there any <u>proofs</u> that you are a Christian?

- The <u>knowledge</u> that God is our heavenly Father
- A new reliance on <u>prayer</u>
- A new ability to understand <u>Scripture</u>
- A new sense of the seriousness of <u>sin</u>
- A new <u>love</u> for lost people
- A new love for <u>other believers</u>

Because I've <u>trusted</u> in Christ's work on the cross.

NOTES

KEY VERSES

One of the most effective ways to drive deeply into our lives the principles we are learning in this series is to memorize key Scriptures. For many, memorization is a new concept or one that has been difficult in the past. We encourage you to stretch yourself and try to memorize these four key verses. If possible, memorize these as a group and make them part of your group time. You may cut these apart and carry them in your wallet.

I have hidden your word in my heart that I might not sin against you.

Psalm 119:11 (NIV)

Session One

For it is by grace you have been saved, through faith—and this not from yourselves, it is the gift of God.

Ephesians 2:8 (NIV)

Session Two

For Christ died for sins once for all, the righteous for the unrighteous, to bring you to God.

1 Peter 3:18a (NIV)

Session Three

"My sheep listen to my voice; I know them, and they follow me. I give them eternal life, and they never perish; no one can snatch them out of my hand."

John 10:27-28 (NIV)

Session Four

Let us draw near to God with a sincere heart in full assurance of faith . . .

Hebrews 10:22a (NIV)

NOTES

We value your thoughts about what you've just read.
Please share them with us. You'll find contact information
in the back of this book.

The Purpose Driven® Life
A six-session video-based study for groups or individuals

Embark on a journey of discovery with this video-based study taught by Rick Warren. In it you will discover the answer to life's most fundamental question: "What on earth am I here for?"

And here's a clue to the answer: It's not about you . . . You were created by God and for God, and until you understand that, life will never make sense. It is only in God that we discover our origin, our identity, our meaning, our purpose, our significance, and our destiny."

Whether you experience this adventure with a small group or on your own, this six-session, video-based study will change your life.

DVD Study Guide: 978-0-310-27866-5
DVD: 978-0-310-27864-1

Be sure to combine this study with your reading of the best-selling book, *The Purpose Driven® Life*, to give you or your small group the opportunity to discuss the implications and applications of living the life God created you to live.

Hardcover, Jacketed: 978-0-310-20571-5
Softcover: 978-0-310-27699-9

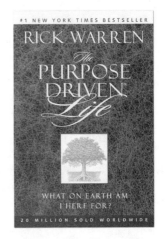

Pick up a copy today at your favorite bookstore!

ZONDERVAN®
.com

Foundations: 11 Core Truths to Build Your Life On

Taught by Tom Holladay and Kay Warren

Foundations is a series of 11 four-week video studies covering the most important, foundational doctrines of the Christian faith. Study topics include:

The Bible—This study focuses on where the Bible came from, why it can be trusted, and how it can change your life.
DVD Study Guide: 978-0-310-27670-8
DVD: 978-0-310-27669-2

God—This study focuses not just on facts about God, but on how to know God himself in a more powerful and personal way.
DVD Study Guide: 978-0-310-27672-2
DVD: 978-0-310-27671-5

Jesus—As we look at what the Bible says about the person of Christ, we do so as people who are developing a lifelong relationship with Jesus.
DVD Study Guide: 978-0-310-27674-6
DVD: 978-0-310-27673-9

The Holy Spirit—This study focuses on the person, the presence, and the power of the Holy Spirit, and how you can be filled with the Holy Spirit on a daily basis.
DVD Study Guide: 978-0-310-27676-0
DVD: 978-0-310-27675-3

Creation—Each of us was personally created by a loving God. This study does not shy away from the great scientific and theological arguments that surround the creation/evolution debate. However, you will find the goal of this study is deepening your awareness of God as your Creator.
DVD Study Guide: 978-0-310-27678-4
DVD: 978-0-310-27677-7

Pick up a copy today at your favorite bookstore!

ZONDERVAN®
.com

Salvation—This study focuses on God's solution to man's need for salvation, what Jesus Christ did for us on the cross, and the assurance and security of God's love and provision for eternity.

DVD Study Guide: 978-0-310-27682-1

DVD: 978-0-310-27679-1

Sanctification—This study focuses on the two natures of the Christian. We'll see the difference between grace and law, and how these two things work in our lives.

DVD Study Guide: 978-0-310-27684-5

DVD: 978-0-310-27683-8

Good and Evil—Why do bad things happen to good people? Through this study we'll see how and why God continues to allow evil to exist. The ultimate goal is to build up our faith and relationship with God as we wrestle with these difficult questions.

DVD Study Guide: 978-0-310-27687-6

DVD: 978-0-310-27686-9

The Afterlife—The Bible does not answer all the questions we have about what happens to us after we die; however, this study deals with what the Bible does tell us. This important study gives us hope and helps us move from a focus on the here and now to a focus on eternity.

DVD Study Guide: 978-0-310-27689-0

DVD: 978-0-310-27688-3

The Church—This study focuses on the birth of the church, the nature of the church, and the mission of the church.

DVD Study Guide: 978-0-310-27692-0

DVD: 978-0-310-27691-3

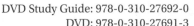

The Second Coming—This study addresses both the hope and the uncertainties surrounding the second coming of Jesus Christ.

DVD Study Guide: 978-0-310-27695-1

DVD: 978-0-310-27693-7

Pick up a copy today at your favorite bookstore!

ZONDERVAN®

.com

Celebrate Recovery, Updated Curriculum Kit

This kit will provide your church with the tools necessary to start a successful Celebrate Recovery program. *Kit includes:*

- Introductory Guide for Leaders DVD
- Leader's Guide
- 4 Participant's Guides (one of each guide)
- CD-ROM with 25 lessons
- CD-ROM with sermon transcripts
- 4-volume audio CD sermon series

Curriculum Kit: 978-0-310-26847-5

Participant's Guide 4-pack

The Celebrate Recovery Participant's Guide 4-pack is a convenient resource when you're just getting started or if you need replacement guides for your program.

Celebrate Recovery Bible

With features based on eight principles Jesus voiced in his Sermon on the Mount, the new *Celebrate Recovery Bible* offers hope, encouragement, and empowerment for those struggling with the circumstances of their lives and the habits they are trying to control.

Hardcover 978-0-310-92849-2
Softcover 978-0-310-93810-1

Pick up a copy today at your favorite bookstore!

ZONDERVAN®
.com

Stepping Out of Denial into God's Grace

Participant's Guide 1 introduces the eight principles of recovery based on Jesus' words in the Beatitudes, and focuses on principles 1–3. Participants learn about denial, hope, sanity, and more.

Getting Right with God, Yourself, and Others

Participant's Guide 3 covers principles 5–7 based on Jesus' words in the Beatitudes. With courage and support from their fellow participants, people seeking recovery will find victory, forgiveness, and grace.

Taking an Honest and Spiritual Inventory

Participant's Guide 2 focuses on the fourth principle based on Jesus' words in the Beatitudes and builds on the Scripture, *"Happy are the pure in heart."* (Matthew 5:8) The participant will learn an invaluable principle for recovery and also take an in-depth spiritual inventory.

Growing in Christ While Helping Others

Participant's Guide 4 walks through the final steps of the eight recovery principles based on Jesus' words in the Beatitudes. In this final phase, participants learn to move forward in newfound freedom in Christ, learning how to give back to others. There's even a practical lesson called "Seven reasons we get stuck in our recoveries."

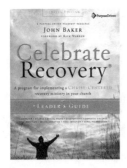

Leader's Guide

The Celebrate Recovery Leader's Guide gives you everything you need to facilitate your preparation time. Virtually walking you through every meeting, the Leader's Guide is a must-have for every leader on your Celebrate Recovery ministry team.

Pick up a copy today at your favorite bookstore!

Wide Angle:
Framing Your Worldview

Christianity is much more than a religion. It is a worldview—a way of seeing all of life and the world around you. Your worldview impacts virtually every decision you make in life: moral decisions, relational decisions, financial decisions— everything. How you see the world determines how you face the world.

In this brand new study, Rick Warren and Chuck Colson discuss such key issues as moral relativism, tolerance, terrorism, creationism vs. Darwinism, sin and suffering. They explore in depth the Christian worldview as it relates to the most important questions in life:

- Why does it matter what I believe?
- How do I know what's true?
- Where do I come from?
- Why is the world so messed up?
- Is there a solution?
- What is my purpose in life?

This study is as deep as it is wide, addressing vitally important topics for every follower of Christ.

DVD Study Guide: 978-1-4228-0083-6
DVD: 978-1-4228-0082-9

Rick Warren

Chuck Colson

The Way of a Worshiper

The pursuit of God is the chase of a lifetime—in fact, it's been going on since the day you were born. The question is: Have you been the hunter or the prey?

This small group study is not about music. It's not even about going to church. It's about living your life as an offering of worship to God. It's about tapping into the source of power to live the Christian life. And it's about discovering the secret to friendship with God.

In these four video sessions, Buddy Owens helps you unpack the meaning of worship. Through his very practical, engaging, and at times surprising insights, Buddy shares truths from Scripture and from life that will help you understand in a new and deeper way just what it means to be a worshiper.

God is looking for worshipers. His invitation to friendship is open and genuine. Will you take him up on his offer? Will you give yourself to him in worship? Then come walk *The Way of a Worshiper* and discover the secret to friendship with God.

DVD Study Guide: 978-1-4228-0096-6
DVD: 978-1-4228-0095-9

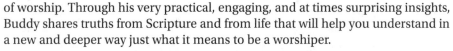

THE WAY of a WORSHIPER

Your study of this material will be greatly enhanced by reading the book, *The Way of a Worshiper: Discover the Secret to Friendship with God.*

Managing Our Finances God's Way

Did you know that there are over 2,350 verses in the Bible about money? Did you know that nearly half of Jesus' parables are about possessions? The Bible is packed with wise counsel about your financial life. In fact, Jesus had more to say about money than about heaven and hell combined.

Introducing a new video-based small group study that will inspire you to live debt free! Created by Saddleback Church and Crown Financial Ministries, learn what the Bible has to say about our finances from Rick Warren, Chip Ingram, Ron Blue, Howard Dayton, and Chuck Bentley as they address important topics like:

- God's Solution to Debt
- Saving and Investing
- Plan Your Spending
- Giving as an Act of Worship
- Enjoy What God Has Given You

Study includes:

- DVD with seven 20-minute lessons

- Workbook with seven lessons

- Resource CD with digital version of all worksheets that perform calculations automatically

- Contact information for help with answering questions

- Resources for keeping financial plans on track and making them lifelong habits

> **NOTE:** PARTICIPANTS DO NOT SHARE PERSONAL FINANCIAL INFORMATION WITH EACH OTHER.

DVD Study Guide: 978-1-4228-0083-6
DVD: 978-1-4228-0082-9

Share Your Thoughts

With the Author: Your comments will be forwarded to the author when you send them to *zauthor@zondervan.com*.

With Zondervan: Submit your review of this book by writing to *zreview@zondervan.com*.

Free Online Resources at
www.zondervan.com/hello

 Zondervan AuthorTracker: Be notified whenever your favorite authors publish new books, go on tour, or post an update about what's happening in their lives.

 Daily Bible Verses and Devotions: Enrich your life with daily Bible verses or devotions that help you start every morning focused on God.

 Free Email Publications: Sign up for newsletters on fiction, Christian living, church ministry, parenting, and more.

 Zondervan Bible Search: Find and compare Bible passages in a variety of translations at www.zondervanbiblesearch.com.

 Other Benefits: Register yourself to receive online benefits like coupons and special offers, or to participate in research.